Ninety-Nine Names of
ALLAH

The Beautiful Names

Shems Friedlander
Al-Hajj Shaikh Muzaffereddin
Calligraphy
Hattat Hamid al-Amidi
Arabic and Turkish Translation
Dr. Tevfik Topuzoglu
(University of Istanbul)

HARPER COLOPHON BOOKS
Harper & Row, Publishers
New York, Hagerstown, San Francisco, London

THE NINETY-NINE NAMES OF ALLAH,
Copyright © 1978 by Shems Friedlander.
Printed in the United States of America.
No part of this book may be used or reproduced in any
manner whatsoever without written permission except
in the case of brief quotations embodied in critical
articles and reviews.
For information address Harper & Row, Publishers, Inc.,
10 East 53rd Street, New York, N.Y. 10022.
Published simultaneously in Canada
by Fitzhenry & Whiteside Limited, Toronto.

First edition: HARPER COLOPHON BOOKS 1978

LIBRARY OF CONGRESS CATALOG NUMBER: 78-19234

ISBN: 0-06-090621-9

This work is dedicated to
my spiritual sons,
Simeon
Joshua
Sirr
and to the memory
of my father
Samuel.
May Allah bless them.

He is Allah, there is no God but Him.

Allah has said
ask from Me through
mentioning
My names.
Hadis Qudsi

FOREWORD

Religious scholars have related that Allah has three thousand Names. One thousand are only known by angels, 1,000 known only by prophets, 300 are in the Torah (Old Testament), 300 are in Zabur (Psalms of David), 300 are in the New Testament, and 99 are in the Qur'an. This makes 2,999 Names. One Name which has been hidden by Allah is called Ism Allah al-a'zam: The Greatest Name of Allah.

All of Allah's Names are great, but since He has hidden this particular Name it is referred to as The Greatest Name. The Name is mentioned in the Qur'an as this Hadis states:

Asma, radiyallahu anha, reports that Prophet Muhammad, peace and blessings of Allah be upon him, said: ''The Greatest Name of Allah is in these two verses of the Qur'an, 'He who is worshipped by you is One God, there is no god but Him, the Compassionate and the Beneficent (sura II,163); also in the first part of sura Ali Imran, Alif Lam Mim--Allah, there is no god but Him, the Alive, the Self-Subsisting.''

Aisha,radiyallahu anha, mentioned that Ya Rab (Oh Lord) is the Greatest Name.

Whoever reads the Qur'an will have read the Greatest Name probably without knowing it. Some of the companions of the Prophet, may the peace and blessings of Allah be upon him, knew the Name. Ali Karramallahu Wachah (the fourth caliph), may Allah exalt him, was one who knew.

Allah has hidden certain things out of His mercy. He has hidden the most righteous people in His eyes (Avliya), so people should respect one another indiscriminately. He has hidden the night of Kadir (the holy night in which Qur'an began to be revealed), and the sura of Kadir (97th chapter) mentions that the night of Kadir is better than 1,000 months. According to Hadis, this night is usually regarded as being the 27th night of Ramadhan. It is hidden so people should act properly and obey His orders throughout Ramadhan.

He has hidden His consent so people will always do good deeds. He has hidden His Greatest Name in the Qur'an so people will read the entire Qur'an.

One should memorize the 99 Names for one's own benefit. However, learning the Names by heart is not the aim. The aim is to find the One who is Named.

There is a Hadis related by Abu Umama which says that the Greatest Name with which prayer is accepted is in these three suras of Qur'an: Al-Baqara, Al-Imran and Taha.

In Al-Baqara the verse is Wa ilahukum ilhum wahid...verse 163.

In Al-Imran the verse is Alif Lam Mim Allahu la ilaha illa huwalhayy al-Qayyum (1,2).

In Taha the verse is Wa'anatilwucuhu...(III).

The Names of Allah are connected with the life of man. All aspects of life can be seen in the Names. When a man is given a Name which relates to one of the 99 Names of Allah it should always be preceded by Abd (servant of).

He who would like to repeat a Name of Allah should first say at least 700 times: La ilaha illa'llah Muhammad Rasulullah (There is no god but God and Muhammad is His Messenger).

To begin, one should clean oneself with a full ablution making certain that all parts of the body are touched by water. If this is not possible one should perform wuzu (the washing of the parts of the body which are generally exposed), as if preparing for prayers. On the days of the repetition one should not eat meat. The place chosen for the repetition should be clean. If these guidelines are observed the answer of Allah could be quick.

Preferably the person should be alone and the repetitions said during the night.

Be warned, ''He who has no knowledge of how to use a sword will injure himself.'' There must be respect, care, and good intentions or an injury could occur. The effect of continuous repetition with bad intention or not according to a way prescribed by a shaikh could cause harm to members of one's household or oneself. This true story of Osman Baba illustrates the point.

Osman Baba repeated Ya-Qahhar (Oh Destroyer) many times until he became obsessed by this Attribute. If he threw a piece of cotton at someone and it hit him, he would die. The people complained to Waliyuddin "Kuddisa Sirruh" who told them to take a piece of cotton and throw it at the back of Osman. When it hit him he turned and said, "Oh Waliyuddin, you have killed me", and he died.

The power was given to him by Allah because he repeated the Name. There are some who want something eagerly or impatiently and attempt to receive it by repetition of the Names without first knowing whether this would be good for them. They keep repeating without knowing. They keep saying *I Want It*. They do not say, "Allah, if it is good for me, let me have it.''

The correct way to the Names is to be on the Right Path. Allah may give to someone who is not on the Right Path but to those on the Right Path He *gives*. If you say these Names and do not receive, it may be that this is not a good thing for you; something not always understood.

While one is repeating a Name there should be no speaking and no interruptions. If thoughts intrude while you are repeating the Name, then remain seated with closed eyes. Make your humility perfect. Imagine that you are dead and the mourners have departed, leaving you alone to face the Judgment. Concentrate all your senses, expel all preoccupations and wayward impulses of the heart and direct your perception toward Allah. Now, continue to repeat the Name.

However, to be interfered with by Shaitan (the Devil) in thoughts may mean that Shaitan found something good in that person in the way of Allah. Faith and righteousness are aspects that Shaitan wishes to prevent in one.

Shaitan is not able to interfere with a person who has reached a certain level with Allah. A beginner in the Way of Allah is more open to the attacks of Shaitan, but he should continue to obey Allah's orders so that he may be free from these attacks and may reach the station of Wali (Friend), or Arif (knows Allah) which is beyond the reach of Shaitan.

Pir Nureddin Jerrahi, may Allah be pleased with him, instructed his murids not to drink water after evening so they would be able to have spiritual dreams. The lessons of the shaikh are given to the dervish according to his dreams. Through these dream interpretations the shaikh knows what lessons to give or to change the Name the dervish might be practicing.

If one drinks an entire bottle of medicine without the prescription of the doctor he will not get better and may even die. The repetition of the Names is the medicine and the shaikh is the doctor. The acuteness of the illness is important, the medicine and the doctor are important, the time that one takes the medicine and the time between taking the medicine are important, and the amount of medicine prescribed is important. The doctor has wisdom of medicine while only Allah has the power to heal.

Yunus Musuli owned a small jewelry shop in the Istanbul bazaar. One day, Pir Nureddin Jerrahi, founder of the Jerrahi Order of Halveti dervishes, walked by the shop and saw the jeweler. He thought the man had an inner light and asked his khalifa whether this man should be taken as a dervish. His khalifa knew the man and said yes.

Pir Nureddin went into the shop. He was eating a peach as he looked around. He repeated a few words, breathed on the peach pit, and it grew and changed into a large, faultless emerald. He asked the jeweler its value. The man was astonished at its size and beauty. "I do not have enough money or property to purchase such a jewel, but I would give all that I have for it," he said.

Pir Nureddin breathed on the emerald and it changed back into the peach pit. "Is this what you would give everything for?" he asked. The jeweler was astonished at what he had witnessed and became a dervish of Pir Nureddin.

Marion

March 18
1983

For my fellow religious
explorer, Carlotta,

with Love from

Harold

Alternate envoi:

for my super-ego
from her infra-ego!

Pir Nureddin said that to make things into gold you must first make your breath gold. The way to do this is to be on the Right Path and study dhikrullah with a shaikh.

Allah hears what is in a person's heart. Whether you speak aloud or have silent words for Allah, there is no difference, for He knows what is in your heart.

The beginning of the path is Allah. The center of the road and the way through is Allah. The end of the path is Allah. That which leads people to disaster is to forget Allah. The tongue mentions dhikr (there is no god but God), but it is the heart that understands.

The Messenger of Allah, may the peace and blessings of Allah be upon him, has said: "There is a piece of flesh in the body. If it is sound, the entire body is sound. If it is unsound, the entire body is unsound. It is the heart."

Allah, who does not fit into heavens or worlds, fits into the hearts of men. The process used to clean the heart is dhikrullah. Dhikr is a key to the secrets of life. When you remember Him and recite His Names standing up, He will remember you when you stand up from your grave. When you ask His forgiveness He will forgive. Allah gives to all because He is Rahman. Not to forget, one has to remember continuously. Mention His Name over that which you eat. If you wish to be near Him become the slave to His slave.

To be far is to have the hope to be near. To be near is to have the taste of fear of being far. This taste of fear is not necessarily suffering.

La ilaha illa'llah (there is no god but God) is the Name of Union. It contains a negation and a confirmation. This is a story that reveals the meaning of la ilaha illa'llah.

There was once a person who knew the truth of God and had reached it through his heart. He appeared no different than any ordinary man. He applied to the religious order and asked them to give him a building for himself and his one murid (student). Those in the office which assigns buildings to shaikhs looked at his poor appearance, tattered clothes, his weakened condition, and failed to see the treasure in his essence. They decided to give a small broken house which they did not know what to do with to this man, so that he might at least repair it and live in it with his one murid.

He accepted the house, repaired the outside and filled the interior with the light of love. Eventually people who could see this light were drawn to him. More and more the house became honored, for the honor of a house is revealed by the dweller.

The office which assigns position and housing became aware of the students crowding around this shaikh whom they did not think much of and decided to test him. He stated his readiness to be examined.

The scholars said that the first lesson of a dervish is "la ilaha illa'llah," and asked him to tell what this meant. He asked if he should give an answer that they expect or should he answer as he really knows it to be. The examiners said that the way they knew was common and that he should tell the way he understands its meaning.

"If you wish the answer the way I understand it, then I cannot do it alone. I ask permission to have with me the one dervish with whom I sought the house."

He sat with his one dervish in front of the religious

scholars and began the dhikr. When he said la ilaha, he disappeared and when he said illa'llah, he reappeared. Again he said la ilaha and disappeared, then said illa'llah and reappeared. The third time he disappeared on la ilaha and reappeared on illa'llah. The fourth time he said la ilaha the entire crowd including the examiners disappeared and when he said illa'llah they all reappeared. Now they understood that under this poor appearance there existed a great treasure. This is the way he showed the meaning of la ilaha illa'llah.

In the following text the commentaries and number of repetitions suggested are open to be altered or determined by the shaikh of an Order. The information given is an introduction to the meanings and effects of the Names. It is advisable to follow the guidance of a shaikh.

The first Name in the text refers to the Attribute of Allah. The repetition preceded by *Ya* refers to the appeal to that Attribute.

Shemseddin Halveti al-Jerrahi
Al-Hajj Shaikh Muzaffereddin

ALLAH

AR-RAḤMĀN

The Beneficent

He who gives blessings and prosperity to all beings without showing disparity.

YA-RAḤMĀN

He who repeats this Name 100 times after each farz [obligatory] prayer will have good memory, a keen awareness, and be free of a heavy heart.

AR-RAHĪM

The Merciful

He who gives blessings and prosperity, particularly to those who use these gifts as Allah has said, and is merciful to the believers in the hereafter.

YA-RAHĪM

He who repeats this Name 100 times after each Fajr [early morning] prayer will find everyone to be friendly towards him and show easiness to him.

AL-MALIK

The Sovereign Lord

He who is the absolute king of the entire universe.

YA-MALIK

He who repeats this Name anytime will be respected and treated accordingly by others.

AL-QUDDŪS

The Holy

He who is free from all error, absentmindedness, is free from incapability and from any kind of defect.

YA-QUDDŪS

The hearts of those who repeat this Name 100 times each day will be free from anxiety.

AS-SALĀM

The Source of Peace

He who frees his servants from all danger and obstruction. He who gives His greeting to those fortunate people in heaven.

YA-SALĀM

He who repeats this Name 160 times to a sick person will help them regain health.

AL-MU'MIN

The Guardian of Faith

He who places faith in the heart of His servants, protects those who seek refuge in Him, and gives tranquility.

YA-MU'MIN

He who repeats this Name will be free from harm.

AL-MUHAYMIN

The Protector

He who watches over and protects all things.

YA-MUHAYMIN

Those who repeat this Name and have complete ablution, their inner being will be luminous.

AL-'AZIZ

The Mighty

The Unconquerable.

YA-'AZIZ

He who repeats this Name 40 times after each Fajr prayer for 40 days will be independent of need from others.

AL-JABBĀR

The Compeller

He who repairs all broken things, who completes that which is incomplete, and who has the ability, with force, to make people do whatever He wants.

YA-JABBĀR

He who repeats this Name will not be compelled to do anything against his wishes, and will not be exposed to violence, severity, or hardness.

AL-MUTAKABBIR

The Majestic

He who shows His greatness in all things and in all ways.

YA-MUTAKABBIR

He who repeats this Name before having intercourse with his wife, Allah will bless him with a righteous child.

AL-KHĀLIQ

The Creator

He who creates everything from nothing and creates all things with the knowledge of what will happen to them.

YA-KHĀLIQ

He who repeats this Name at night, Allah will create an angel whose duty it is to act righteously for this person until the day of judgment. The reward for this angel's actions will be given to that person.

AL-BĀRI'

The Evolver

He who creates all things in proportion.

AL-MUṢAWWIR

The Fashioner

He who designs all things.

YA-KHĀLIQ, YA-BĀRI',

YA-MUṢAWWIR

If a woman who desires to give birth, but cannot, fasts seven days, and each day at the breaking of the fast [if-tar] she repeats these three Names twenty-one times, breathes into a glass of water, and then breaks the fast with this water, Allah will bless her with a child.

AL-GHAFFĀR

The Forgiver

He who is all-forgiving.

YA-GHAFFĀR

He who repeats this Name will be forgiven his sins.

AL-QAHHĀR

The Subduer

He who is victorious and dominant in a way that He can do anything He wills.

YA-QAHHĀR

The soul of him who repeats this Name will conquer the desires of the flesh, and his heart will be made free from the attractions of the world and gain inner peace. This Name also frees one from being wronged.

AL-WAHHĀB

The Bestower

He who donates all blessings to His creatures.

YA-WAHHĀB

The person who repeats this Name seven times after [dua] appealing to Allah, his appeal will be answered. He who has a desire, or a person who is captured by an enemy, or someone who can't earn enough to maintain himself, if he repeats this Name for three or seven nights 100 times after two rak'as [prayers] at midnight with ablution, Allah will bless him with all his needs.

AR-RAZZĀQ

The Provider

He who provides all things beneficial to His creatures.

YA-RAZZĀQ

He who repeats this Name will be provided with sustenance by Allah.

AL-FATTĀḤ

The Opener

He who opens the solution to all problems, and eliminates obstacles.

YA-FATTĀḤ

The heart of him who repeats this Name will be open, and he will be given victory.

AL-'ALĪM

The All-Knowing

He who is all-knowing.

YA-'ALĪM

He who repeats this Name, his heart will become luminous, revealing divine light [Nur].

AL-QĀBIḌ

The Constrictor

He who constricts.

YA-QĀBIḌ

He who writes this Name on 50 pieces of food [fruit, bread, etc.] for 40 days will be free from hunger.

AL-BĀSIṬ

The Expander

He who is the expander.

YA-BĀSIṬ

He who repeats this name ten times during Fajr with open hands [palms up], then rubs his face with his hands, will be free of need from others.

AL-KHĀFIḌ

The Abaser

He who diminishes or decreases.

YA-KHĀFIḌ

Those who fast three days, and on the fourth day in a gathering read this Name 70,000 times, Allah will free them from harm by their enemy.

AR-RĀFI'

The Exalter

He who uplifts.

YA-RĀFI'

He who repeats this Name 100 times day and night, Allah will make him higher as far as honor, richness and merit are concerned.

AL-MU'IZZ

The Honorer

He who makes one glorious, gives dignity, and treats one with respect.

YA-MU'IZZ

Repeated 140 times after Isha prayer during Monday and Friday nights [according to the lunar calendar, Sunday and Thursday], Allah makes him dignified in the eyes of others. That person will have fear of no one but Allah.

AL-MUZILL

The Dishonorer

He who lowers and puts one in abasement and degradation.

YA-MUZILL

He who repeats this Name 75 times will be free from harm by those who are jealous of him and wish to harm him. Allah will protect him.

AS-SAMĪ'

The All-Hearing

He who hears everything.

YA-SAMĪ'

He who repeats this Name 100 times without speaking to anyone on Thursdays after the Zuhr prayer [noon-time], Allah will bestow on him any desire.

AL-BAṢĪR

The All-Seeing

He who sees everything.

YA-BAṢĪR

He who repeats this Name 100 times between farz and the first sunnet prayer at Cuma [Friday afternoon prayer], Allah will give this person esteem in the eyes of others.

AL-ḤAKAM

The Judge

He who judges and provides what is due.

YA-ḤAKAM

He who repeats this Name many times at night, many secrets [sirr] will be revealed to him.

AL-'ADL

The Just

The just one.

YA-'ADL

On Friday night, if you write this Name on a piece of bread, people will obey you.

AL-LAṬĪF

The Subtle One

He who knows the delicate meanings of everything. He who creates things most subtly, which cannot be understood by people, and He who gives blessings to people in the most subtle ways.

YA-LAṬĪF

He who has become poor, and is lonely, if he repeats this Name 100 times after two rak'as [extra prayers], his desires will be fulfilled.

AL-KHABĪR

The Aware

He who has knowledge of the most secret parts of everything, and knows their inner meanings.

YA-KHABĪR

He who has a bad habit which he does not like, and continuously repeats this Name, will be quickly freed from this habit.

AL-ḤALĪM

The Forbearing One

He who is clement.

YA-ḤALĪM

If one writes this Name on a piece of paper, and puts it where his seed is sown, no harm, disaster or calamity will befall his crop.

AL-'AẒĪM

The Great One

He who is magnificent.

YA-'AẒĪM

Those who repeat this Name many times will be respected.

AL-GHAFŪR

The All-Forgiving

He who forgives all.

YA-GHAFŪR

He who has a headache, fever, and is despondent, who continuously repeats this Name, will be relieved of his ailment.

ASH-SHAKŪR

The Appreciative

He who is grateful and gives rewards for deeds done for Him.

YA-SHAKŪR

He who has a heavy heart, and repeats this Name 41 times, breathes into a glass of water, then washes his face with this water, his heart will lighten, and he will be able to maintain himself.

AL-'ALĪ

The Most High

He who is most high.

YA-'ALĪ

He whose faith is low and repeats this Name, it will be raised, his destiny will be opened; the traveler will reach his homeland.

AL-KABĪR

The Most Great

He who is most great.

YA-KABĪR

He who repeats this Name 100 times each day will have esteem.

AL-ḤAFĪẒ

The Preserver

He who preserves all things in detail, and for a time preserves them from misfortune and calamity.

YA-ḤAFĪẒ

He who repeats this Name 16 times each day will be protected against calamities.

AL-MUQĪT

The Maintainer

He who sustains.

YA-MUQĪT

If someone with a bad-mannered child repeats this Name into a glass of water, and gives this water to the child to drink, the child will have good manners.

AL-ḤASĪB

The Reckoner

He who knows in detail the account of things people do throughout their lives.

YA-ḤASĪB

If one is afraid of being robbed, afraid of the jealousy of another, of being harmed or wronged, he begins on a Thursday to repeat this Name 70 times, day and night, for seven days and nights. At the seventy-first time, he says Allah is my Reckoner [Habiyallah-ul-Hasib], and he will be free of his fears.

AL-JALĪL

The Sublime One

He who has wealth, dominion and holiness.

YA-JALĪL

He who writes this Name on a piece of paper with musk and saffron, washes it, and drinks the water from a ceramic container made of earth, will be revered among men.

AL-KARĪM

The Generous One

He who is generous.

YA-KARĪM

He who repeats this Name many times will have esteem in this world and the hereafter.

AR-RAQĪB

The Watchful

He who observes all creatures, and every action is under His control.

YA-RAQĪB

He who repeats this Name seven times on himself, his family and property, all will be under Allah's protection.

AL-MUJĪB

The Responsive

The One who responds to every need.

YA-MUJĪB

The appeal of him who repeats this Name will be answered.

AL WĀSI'

The All-Embracing

He who has limitless capacity and abundance.

YA-WĀSI'

If one who has difficulty earning, repeats this Name, he will have good earnings.

AL-ḤAKĪM

The Wise

He who has wisdom in all orders and actions.

YA-ḤAKĪM

He who repeats this Name continuously [from time to time] will not have difficulties in his work.

AL-WADŪD

The Loving

He who loves those who do good and bestows on them His compassion. He who is the only one who should be loved and whose friendship is to be earned.

YA-WADŪD

If there is a quarrel between two people, and one of them repeats this Name 1,000 times over some food and has the other person eat the food, there will be no disagreement between them.

AL-MAJĪD

The Most Glorious One

He who is most glorious.

YA-MAJĪD

He who repeats this Name gains glory.

AL-BĀ'ITH

The Resurrector

He who gives life to all creatures on the judgment day.

YA-BĀ'ITH

He who repeats this Name gains the fear of Allah.

ASH-SHAHĪD

The Witness

He who is present everywhere and observes all things.

YA-SHAHĪD

He who has a rebellious child and repeats this Name to
the child, the child will be obedient.

AL-ḤAQQ

The Truth

He whose existence has no change.

YA-ḤAQQ

If one has lost something and repeats this Name, he will find what is lost.

AL-WAKĪL

The Trustee

He who provides a means to solve all problems in the best way.

YA-WAKĪL

He who is afraid of drowning, being burnt in a fire, or any similar danger, and repeats this Name continuously [from time to time], will be under the protection of Allah.

AL-QAWĪ

The Most Strong

YA-QAWĪ

He who cannot defeat his enemy, and repeats this Name with the intention of not being harmed, will be free from his enemy's harm.

AL-MATĪN

The Firm One

YA-MATĪN

If one has troubles and repeats this Name, his troubles will disappear.

AL-WALĪ

The Protecting Friend

He who is the Friend of His righteous servants.

YA-WALĪ

He who repeats this Name is likely to be a waliullah, the friend of Allah.

AL-ḤAMĪD

The Praiseworthy

He who is the only one to be praised and glorified and thanked by all creatures.

YA-ḤAMĪD

He who repeats this Name will be loved and praised.

AL-MUḤṢĪ

The Reckoner

He who knows the number of all things although they cannot be counted, and knows each of them.

YA-MUḤṢĪ

He who is afraid of being questioned on the judgment day, and repeats this Name 1,000 times, will have easiness.

AL-MUBDĪ

The Originator

He who has created for the first time all beings from nothing and without any model.

YA-MUBDĪ

If this Name is repeated and breathed toward a pregnant woman who is afraid of aborting, she will be free of danger.

AL-MU‘ĪD

The Restorer

He who restores all beings.

YA-MU‘ĪD

If this Name is repeated 70 times for someone who is away from his family, that person will return safely.

AL-MUḤYĪ

The Giver of Life

He who gives life and health.

YA-MUḤYĪ

If a person has a heavy burden and repeats this Name seven times each day, his burden will be taken away.

AL-MUMĪT

The Creator of Death

He who creates death.

YA-MUMĪT

This Name is repeated to destroy one's enemy.

AL-ḤAYY

The Alive

He is all-knowing and His strength is sufficient for everything.

YA-ḤAYY

He who repeats this Name will have long life.

AL-QAYYŪM

The Self-Subsisting

He who holds the entire universe.

YA-QAYYŪM

He who repeats this Name will not fall into inadvertency.

AL-WĀJID

The Finder

He who finds whatever He wants in the time He desires.

YA-WĀJID

He who repeats this Name will have richness of heart.

AL-MĀJID

The Noble

He whose highness is great, who is beneficent, and His munificence is rich.

YA-MĀJID

He who repeats this Name, his heart will be enlightened.

AL-WĀHID

The Unique

He who is One in His actions, His Names, who has no partner or equal in His attributes, personality, and orders.

YA-WĀHID

He who repeats this Name alone and in a quiet place will be free from fear and delusion.

AL-AHAD

The One

YA-AHAD

He who repeats this Name 1,000 times will have certain secrets opened to him.

AṢ-ṢAMAD

The Eternal

He who is the only being to apply to if one has any
need to be completed or any troubles to be eliminated.

YA-ṢAMAD

He who repeats this Name many times, Allah will
provide his needs, and as a result he will not need
others, but they will need him.

AL-QĀDIR

The Able

He who is able to do anything in the way He wills.

YA-QĀDIR

He who repeats this Name, all his desires will be fulfilled.

AL-MUQTADIR

The Powerful

He who is more powerful than any being.

YA-MUQTADIR

He who repeats this Name will be aware of the truth.

AL-MUQADDIM

The Expediter

YA-MUQADDIM

He who repeats this Name on the battlefield, or who has fear of being alone in an awe-inspiring place, no harm will come to him.

AL-MU'AKHKHIR

The Delayer

He who delays whatever He wants.

YA-MU'AKHKHIR

He who repeats this Name in his heart 100 times each day, only love of Allah will remain. No other love can enter.

AL-AWWAL

The First

YA-AWWAL

He who would like to have a child, or would like to
come together with a person who is traveling, repeats
this Name 1,000 times for 40 Fridays.

AL-ĀKHIR

The Last

YA-ĀKHIR

He who repeats this Name many times will lead a good life and at the end of this life will have a good death.

AZ-ẒĀHIR

The Manifest

YA-ẒĀHIR

He who recites this Name 15 times after Friday [Cuma] prayer, divine light [Nur] will enter his heart.

AL-BĀṬIN

The Hidden

YA-BĀṬIN

He who repeats this Name three times each day will be
able to see the truth in things.

AL-WĀLI

The Governor

He who directs, manages, conducts, governs, measures, plans every action which happens at any moment in the entire universe.

YA-WĀLI

He who repeats this Name and breathes it into his house, his house will be free from danger.

AL-MUTA'ĀLĪ

The Most Exalted

He who is higher than any action, manner or condition, and any thought that any being may have. This Name indicates that Allah is higher than the most evolved thought of man.

YA-MUTA'ĀLĪ

He who repeats this Name many times will gain the benevolence of Allah.

AL-BARR

The Source of All Goodness

He who is tolerant to His servants, to all creatures, and is good to them.

YA-BARR

He who repeats this Name to his child, this child will be free from misfortune.

AT-TAWWĀB

The Acceptor of Repentance

YA-TAWWĀB

He who repeats this Name many times, his repentance will be accepted.

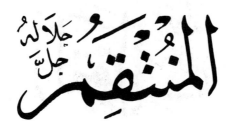

AL-MUNTAQIM

The Avenger

He who punishes wrongdoers.

YA-MUNTAQIM

He who repeats this Name many times will be victorious against his enemies.

AL-'AFUW

The Pardoner

He who pardons all who repent sincerely as if they had no previous sin.

YA-'AFUW

He who repeats this Name many times, all his sins will be forgiven.

AR-RA'ŪF

The Compassionate

He who is benign.

YA-RA'ŪF

He who repeats this Name many times will be blessed by Allah.

MĀLIK-UL-MULK

The Eternal Owner of Sovereignty

YA-MĀLIK-AL-MULK

He who repeats this Name will have esteem among people.

DHŪL-JALĀL-WAL-IKRĀM

The Lord of Majesty and Bounty

YA-DHŪL-JALĀL-WAL-IKRĀM

He who repeats this Name many times will be rich.

AL-MUQSIṬ

The Equitable

He who does His work accordingly and in a balanced way.

YA-MUQSIṬ

He who repeats this Name will be free from the harm of the devil.

AL-JĀME'

The Gatherer

He who collects things, gathers them, anywhere He wants, at any time.

YA-JĀME'

He who repeats this Name will find the things that he lost.

AL-GHANĪ

The Self-Sufficient

YA-GHANĪ

He who repeats this Name will be contented and not covetous.

AL-MUGHNĪ

The Enricher

YA-MUGHNĪ

He who repeats this Name ten times for ten Fridays will become self-sufficient.

AL-MĀNI'

The Preventer

YA-MĀNI'

Those who repeat this Name will have a good family life.

AD-ḌĀRR

The Distresser

He who creates that which makes one despondent.

YA-ḌĀRR

Those who are in a low class, if they repeat this Name on Friday nights, their status will be raised.

AN-NĀFI‘

The Propitious

He who creates all things which provide goodness and benefit.

YA-NĀFI‘

He who repeats this Name for four days as many times as he can, no harm will come to him.

AN-NŪR

The Light

He who provides divine light to the entire universe; to the faces, minds and hearts of His servants.

YA-NŪR

Those who repeat this Name will have inner light.

AL-HĀDĪ

The Guide

He who guides, gives success and directs His servant to do things beneficial to others.

YA-HĀDĪ

He who repeats this Name will have spiritual knowledge.

AL-BADĪ'

The Incomparable

He who creates wonders in the universe without any design.

YA-BADĪ'

He who repeats this Name 70 times in the following way, all his troubles will disappear:
Ya Badee'i as-semavati wal-ard [Oh He who is the creator of incomparable things on earth and in the universe].

AL-BĀQĪ

The Everlasting

YA-BĀQĪ

He who repeats this Name 100 times before sunrise will be free from all disasters throughout his life, and will be shown mercy in the hereafter.

AL-WĀRITH

The Supreme Inheritor

He who has everlasting ownership of all things. Finite man only has temporary ownership, and at death all creatures have nothing.

YA-WĀRITH

He who repeats this Name will have long life.

AR-RASHĪD

The Guide to the Right Path

He who is the guide, with wisdom, to the right path according to His eternal plan.

YA-RASHĪD

He who repeats this Name 1,000 times between early evening prayer [Maghrib] and night prayer [Isha], his troubles will be cleared up.

AṢ-ṢABŪR

The Patient

YA-ṢABŪR

He who is in any trouble, difficulty or sorrow and repeats this Name 3,000 times, will be rescued from his difficulty.

Allah has said
pray to Me, so
that I will
answer you.

AR-RAḤMĀN

The Beneficent

AR-RAḤĪM

The Merciful

AL-MALIK

The Sovereign Lord

AL-QUDDŪS

The Holy

AS-SALĀM

The Source of Peace

AL-MU'MIN

The Guardian of Faith

AL-MUHAYMIN

The Protector

AL-'AZIZ

The Mighty

AL-JABBĀR

The Compeller

AL-MUTAKABBIR

The Majestic

AL-KHĀLIQ

The Creator

AL-BĀRI'

The Evolver

AL-MUṢAWWIR	AL-ʿALĪM
The Fashioner	The All-Knowing
AL-GHAFFĀR	AL-QĀBIḌ
The Forgiver	The Constrictor
AL-QAHHĀR	AL-BĀSIṬ
The Subduer	The Expander
AL-WAHHĀB	AL-KHĀFIḌ
The Bestower	The Abaser
AR-RAZZĀQ	AR-RĀFIʿ
The Provider	The Exalter
AL-FATTĀḤ	AL-MUʿIZZ
The Opener	The Honorer

AL-MUZILL	AL-KHABĪR
The Dishonorer	The Aware
AS-SAMĪ'	AL-ḤALĪM
The All-Hearing	The Forbearing One
AL-BAṢĪR	AL-'AẒĪM
The All-Seeing	The Great One
AL-ḤAKAM	AL-GHAFŪR
The Judge	The All-Forgiving
AL-'ADL	ASH-SHAKŪR
The Just	The Appreciative
AL-LAṬĪF	AL-'ALĪ
The Subtle One	The Most High

AL-KABĪR	AR-RAQĪB
The Most Great	The Watchful
AL-ḤAFĪẒ	AL-MUJĪB
The Preserver	The Responsive
AL-MUQĪT	AL WĀSI'
The Maintainer	The All-Embracing
AL-ḤASĪB	AL-ḤAKĪM
The Reckoner	The Wise
AL-JALĪL	AL-WADŪD
The Sublime One	The Loving
AL-KARĪM	AL-MAJĪD
The Generous One	The Most Glorious One

AL-BĀ'ITH

The Resurrector

ASH-SHAHĪD

The Witness

AL-ḤAQQ

The Truth

AL-WAKĪL

The Trustee

AL-QAWĪ

The Most Strong

AL-MATĪN

The Firm One

AL-WALĪ

The Protecting Friend

AL-ḤAMĪD

The Praiseworthy

AL-MUḤṢĪ

The Reckoner

AL-MUBDĪ

The Originator

AL-MU'ĪD

The Restorer

AL-MUḤYĪ

The Giver of Life

AL-MUMĪT

The Creator of Death

AL-ḤAYY

The Alive

AL-QAYYŪM

The Self-Subsisting

AL-WĀJID

The Finder

AL-MĀJID

The Noble

AL-WĀHID

The Unique

AL-AḤAD

The One

AṢ-ṢAMAD

The Eternal

AL-QĀDIR

The Able

AL-MUQTADIR

The Powerful

AL-MUQADDIM

The Expediter

AL-MU'AKHKHIR

The Delayer

AL-AWWAL

The First

AL-ĀKHIR

The Last

AẒ-ẒĀHIR

The Manifest

AL-BĀṬIN

The Hidden

AL-WĀLI

The Governor

AL-MUTA'ĀLĪ

The Most Exalted

AL-BARR

The Source of All Goodness

AT-TAWWĀB

The Acceptor of Repentance

AL-MUNTAQIM

The Avenger

AL-'AFUW

The Pardoner

AR-RA'ŪF

The Compassionate

MĀLIK-UL-MULK

The Eternal Owner of Sovereignty

DHŪL-JALĀL-WAL-IKRĀM

The Lord of Majesty and Bounty

AL-MUQSIṬ

The Equitable

AL-JĀME' The Gatherer	AL-HĀDĪ The Guide
AL-GHANĪ The Self-Sufficient	AL-BADĪ' The Incomparable
AL-MUGHNĪ The Enricher	AL-BĀQĪ The Everlasting
AL-MĀNI' The Preventer	AL-WĀRITH The Supreme Inheritor
AD-DĀRR The Distresser	AR-RASHĪD The Guide to the Right Path
AN-NĀFI' The Propitious	AS-SABŪR The Patient
AN-NŪR The Light